D1526496

A Tale of TWO KINGS

GOD'S STORY OF REDEMPTION

Gloria Furman

ARTWORK BY *Natalia Moore*

HARVEST HOUSE PUBLISHERS
EUGENE, OREGON

A long, long time ago—
actually, before there was time—
there was God.

And then one day, God
created days. He created
everything you can see...
and everything
you can't see.

God made people to be his representatives, to do his will, and to show the universe what he is like. People are God's most special creation!

The first person God
made was a man
named Adam.

God gave Adam a special job—the kind of work a king would do! His job was to take care of a beautiful garden and to fill the earth with more people to be God's representatives.

Of course, Adam couldn't do this job by himself. In fact, God never meant for Adam to be alone! From Adam's rib, God made his wife, Eve.

God gave Adam and Eve
everything they needed
to be the people God
created them to be.

Adam and Eve loved God!
They were so happy and fearless
and strong! But then something
went wrong, and people began
to feel sad and scared or get
sick and eventually die, just
like people do today

What happened?

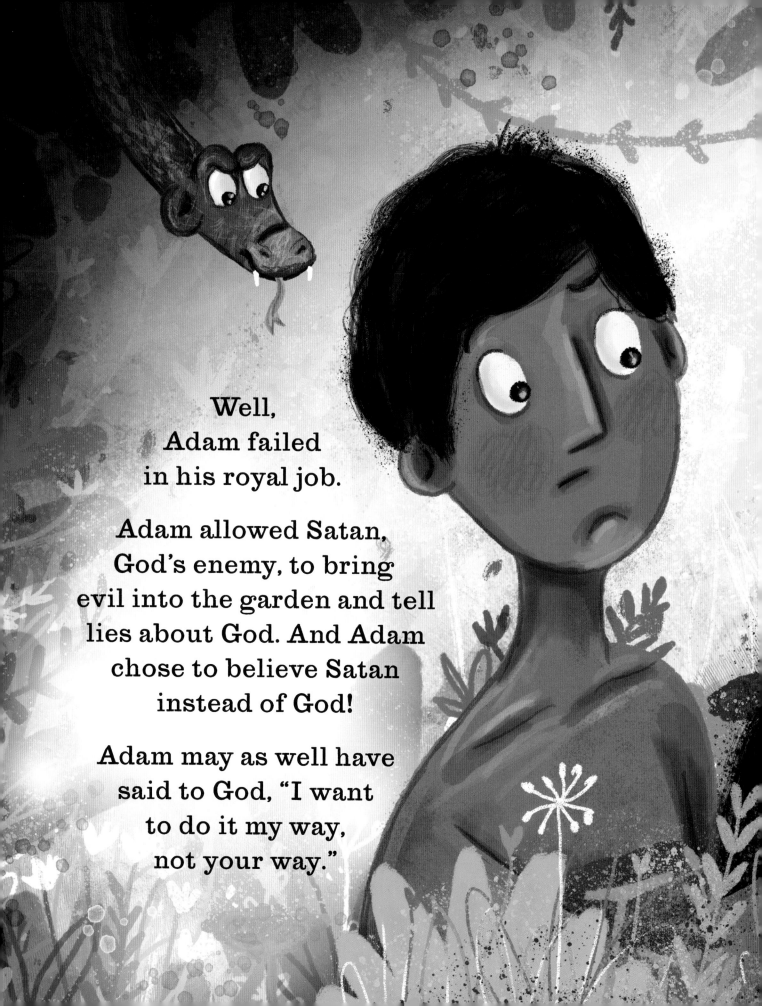

Well,
Adam failed
in his royal job.

Adam allowed Satan,
God's enemy, to bring
evil into the garden and tell
lies about God. And Adam
chose to believe Satan
instead of God!

Adam may as well have
said to God, "I want
to do it my way,
not your way."

Adam had turned away
from God (that's called "sin").
Now everyone born after him—
including you and me—
is born into sin.

But because we are
so very precious to God,
he promised he would send
another man to help us be
friends with God again.

This man would be greater than Adam.
He would be a new King and would undo
what Adam had messed up. He would perfectly
obey God's Word, deliver God's people from their
sin, defeat God's enemy, and finish the job of
filling the earth with people who show
the universe what God is like.

This new King would
bring us back to God.

But before the new King was born, years and years went by. Millions of people were born after Adam, and God used some of them to help rescue his people from their everyday problems.

But there was still one big problem...
everyone's friendship with God was
still broken because of sin.

At long last, in God's perfect timing,
God sent the new King from heaven to earth.
It was his one and only Son, Jesus!

Jesus would be the way for people
to be God's friends again and live with
him forever. Jesus would forgive our sin,
conquer God's enemy, fill the earth with people
who show the universe what God is like,
and someday make all things new.

One day, Satan came to Jesus and told him to turn away from God, just as he had told Adam to turn away from God so long ago.

Would Jesus pass
the same test Adam
had failed?

Jesus refused to
turn away from God.
Jesus remembered God's
Word, and he did not
believe Satan's lies.

Another time, Jesus went to a garden to pray. He knew he was about to give up his life on the cross. Jesus knew this was the only way to pay for the sin of everyone who trusts in him so they could be friends with God again.

In that garden,
Jesus prayed to his Father,
"I'm willing to do this your way,
not my way."

Jesus hadn't done anything wrong, but he was killed on a cross like a dangerous criminal. After Jesus died, his friends put his body in a tomb in a garden.

Three days later, some women went to
the garden to help take care of Jesus's body.
But God had raised Jesus from the dead!

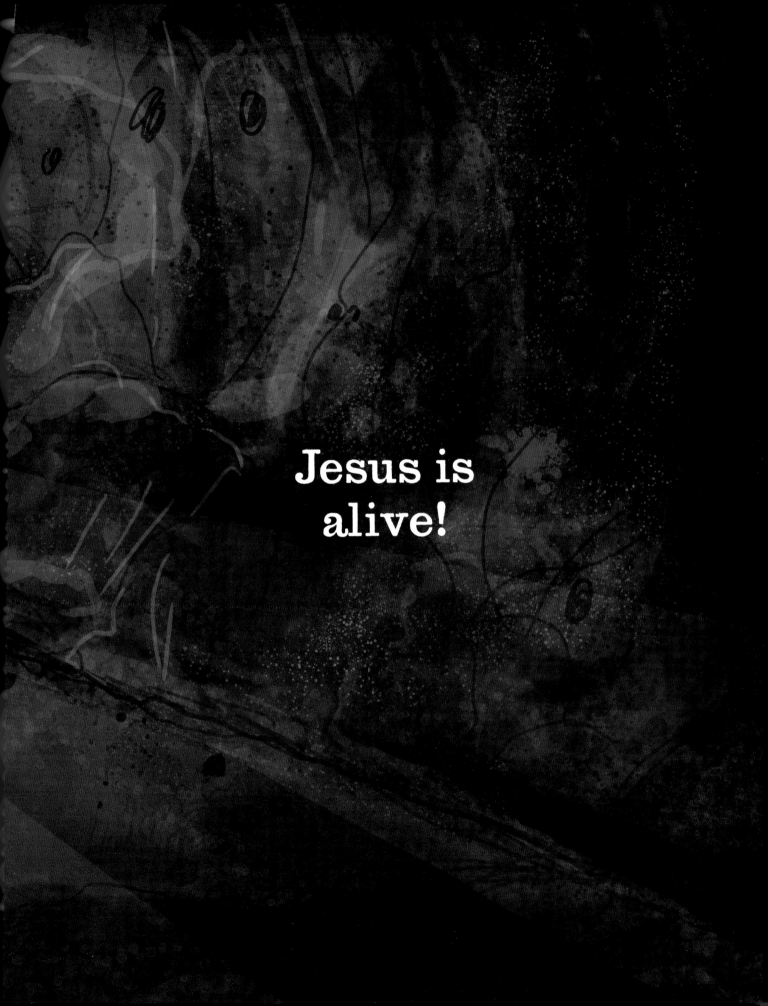

Jesus is
alive!

Through Adam's one act of disobedience, we were all made into sinners.

Through Jesus's obedience on the cross, everyone who trusts in him will be made righteous.

In Adam, we all died.

In Jesus, we are made alive.

Jesus the King is alive today, and he is still doing the job his Father gave him to do. Jesus is filling the world with more and more people who show the universe what God is like.

Where?
Everywhere!
All over the
world!

And someday, when Jesus comes back,
he will raise our bodies from the dead, too.
He will make a new creation where
we'll live with him forever.

That means that we have nothing to fear. Instead, we can have great hope! Jesus is greater than everything scary and sad—he is greater than all the world. We can trust Jesus, the King who is making all things new.

A Word to Parents

Children tend to know a whole lot more than we think they do. However, what is not obvious to them (and us) is where to place our hope. We need real, reliable hope—hope that is more glorious and more certain than the promise of dessert if you eat all your supper.

One of my favorite theologians, Herman Bavinck, said, "This is a world full of humor, laughter mixed with tears, existing in the sign of the cross, and given immediately after the fall to Christ, the Man of sorrows, that he might save and subdue it." Kids and adults know the world is not the way it should be. We see the humor and taste the bitter tears. But what we don't always see or remember is that Jesus Christ is the most deserving of our hope and trust.

I hope this little book helps you and your kids see the glory and trustworthiness of Jesus, the King who died and rose so that we could live with him forever.

Cover design by Juicebox Designs

Interior design by Left Coast Design

A Tale of Two Kings

Text copyright © 2021 by Gloria Furman.

Artwork copyright © 2021 by Natalia Moore

Published by Harvest House Publishers

Eugene, Oregon 97408

www.harvesthousepublishers.com

HARVEST KIDS is a trademark of The Hawkins Children's LLC. Harvest House
Publishers, Inc., is the exclusive licensee of the trademark HARVEST KIDS.

ISBN 978-0-7369-8022-7 (hardcover)

Library of Congress Cataloging-in-Publication Data Record is available at
https://lccn.loc.gov/2020003431.

Printed in China

20 21 22 23 24 25 26 27 28 / LP / 10 9 8 7 6 5 4 3 2 1